37

WAYS TO BOOST YOUR COACHING PRACTICE

STEVE CHANDLER

PLUS: THE 17 LIES THAT HOLD COACHES BACK AND THE TRUTH THAT SETS THEM FREE!

37

WAYS TO BOOST YOUR COACHING PRACTICE

STEVE CHANDLER

PLUS: THE 17 LIES THAT HOLD COACHES BACK AND THE TRUTH THAT SETS THEM FREE!

MAURICE BASSETT

books for athletes of the mind

37 Ways to BOOST Your Coaching Practice

Copyright © 2015 by Steve Chandler

Maurice Bassett
P.O. Box 839
Anna Maria, FL 34216-0839

Contact the publisher:
MauriceBassett@gmail.com
www.MauriceBassett.com

Contact the author:
www.SteveChandler.com

Editing by Kathryn McCormick and Chris Nelson
Cover design by Carrie Brito

ISBN-978-1-60025-028-6

Library of Congress Control Number 2015903991

First Edition

To Kathy, Maurice,
and the angels of the ACS

Contents

Part One

37 Ways to BOOST Your Coaching Practice

Introduction: Why does coaching matter? 3

1. Time to dance with the universe 7
2. Act proud of your professional skill 9
3. Do it for the love of it all 11
4. Leave the conceptual world behind 13
5. Don't be afraid to jump 15
6. Take two steps for beginning success 17
7. Practice the power of truth 19
8. Be sure to challenge the YES 21
9. Don't forget to coach 23
10. When you have a successful call or visit, DON'T STOP! 25
11. Learn from the world's best coaches 27
12. Stop scaring people away 29
13. Uncover the other person's belief 31
14. Stop complexifying your own future 33
15. Focus on the other person's world 35
16. Stop thinking about what they're thinking 37
17. Stop selling and start serving 39
18. Learn to relax another person 41
19. Improve your conversations 43
20. Express your loving curiosity 45
21. Slow down and dive deep 47
22. Roll up your sleeves and go to work 51
23. Master the practice of story-telling 53
24. Look for problems, not clients 57
25. Get ready to get real 59
26. Use this code to get clients 61
27. Stop talking people into coaching 63
28. Do what has you helping people now 65
29. Pump more time and love into it 67

30. Stop worrying about your value.. 69
31. Help them transcend the hidden fear 71
32. Don't be afraid of a spouse 75
33. Just have that one talk today 77
34. Don't make this a horror movie 79
35. Stop impressing your friends 81
36. Make your fee sound good to *you*...................................... 83
37. Keep it simple, keep it clean 87

Part Two

The 17 Lies Coaches Tell Themselves
(until they wake up)

Introduction: Truth is the most advanced client system *of all*...... 93

Lie #1:   It's who you know.. 97
Lie #2:   There's something wrong with me............................. 101
Lie #3:   I'm too old for that 105
Lie #4:   I can't because I'm afraid... 111
Lie #5:   What doesn't kill me makes me stronger 117
Lie #6:   There's nothing I can do... 121
Lie #7:   I worry because I care 125
Lie #8:   I'm sadder now, but wiser... 129
Lie #9:   The longer I have a habit, the harder it is to break...... 133
Lie #10: People really upset me.. 137
Lie #11: Winning the lottery would solve everything............... 143
Lie #12: They're too beautiful for this world 149
Lie #13: You hurt my self-esteem 153
Lie #14: It's a shame we didn't capture that on video............... 157
Lie #15: That's just the way I am 161
Lie #16: I'd love to do that, but I don't have the time............... 167
Lie #17: I'm helpless 173

About the author 177
Books by Steve Chandler 179
Audio by Steve Chandler.. 181
The Coaching Prosperity School and
  its Advanced Client Systems... 183
Bonus chapters from Wealth Warrior 185

The most beautiful fate, the most wonderful good fortune that can happen to any human being, is to be paid for doing that which he passionately loves to do.

~ Abraham H. Maslow

Part One

37 Ways to BOOST
Your Coaching Practice

Introduction

Why does coaching matter?

*According to Career Partners International, 40% of 400
U.S. and Canadian business leaders interviewed chose
coaching as their preferred method for leadership
development. Research is accumulating that shows a
return-on-investment (ROI) of five to eight
times the cost of coaching, or 500%-800%.*

David Rock and Linda J. Page
Coaching with the Brain in Mind

Notice how the outside world finds it to be a startling
NEWSFLASH that coaching is now recognized as **the
best thing a leader can do** to improve professional
development.

Those of us who have been coached already know the
impact of coaching. Our lives have been changed
profoundly.

We also know that *anyone* who chooses to be great at
what they do (including living a good life) will benefit by
choosing a coach.

Any actor needing to learn a character for a film shoot
will have a personal dialect coach (see *The King's Speech*

for the value of coaching). Any athlete wanting to go to the next level has at least one coach to get him or her there. All the singers entering the semi-finals of *American Idol* and *The Voice* have coaches. All of them—which is 100%, not 40%.

So maybe it's not surprising that coaching is actually worth it.

Everyone has always said that two heads are better than one.

Be a lamp, or a lifeboat or a ladder.
Help someone's soul heal.
Walk out of your house like a shepherd.

~ Rumi

Chapter 1

Time to dance with the universe

I'll rip a tree
out of the ground
and flip it upside down
before I turn over
a new leaf, clown!

Eminem
White Trash Party

Coaching is about change. When you get a prospect on the line, you will do well to focus on what they want to change. Instead of what most coaches do: they focus on themselves. They focus on fees and tactics and strategies for persuasion.

That does not work.

Stay with the possibility for change.

Change scares people, even though it's only always the best thing.

Especially personal change. As in turning over a new leaf.

Zen masters ask their students to meditate upon the

beauty of impermanence. Then to meditate upon its eternal being.

The best businesses follow this credo:

CHANGE BEFORE YOU HAVE TO.

The best people do, too.

The whole idea of nailing things down and securing them is the root cause of anxiety and misery.

Dance with change... In other words: dance with the universe. The soul is not a static thing. The soul becomes. Life is better than we think at any given time. Life is crazy good.

Chapter 2

Act proud of your professional skill

There came a wonderful moment in my life when I stopped all my workday friendship-seeking behavior and chose, instead, to turn pro.

What about you? Are you giving a lot of free advice to people in your world? Do people take you to lunch because you always have such great advice for them?

Do you get your sense of personal significance from "helping" all these people (even when you notice they rarely follow your advice)?

Stop doing it. That would be the tip I'd give you if I only had one tip to give.

Other tips?

Well, are people *asking* for all this advice? If so, do they know you're a coach and do this advice thing professionally?

It's certainly okay to love people and really help them.

But if I have a professional service I'm proud of (and only proud because of all the time I devote to making it masterful—like you do—watching videos more than once, reading books more than once, going to seminars and listening to webinars more than once, coaching people all day) then I want my service delivered professionally, and not as a social gesture of friendship.

Just like a doctor would not go around swabbing people at a dinner party. He wouldn't walk up to you and say, "I'd love to operate on you."

My best practice to break the addiction to advice-giving is to just listen to people quietly and *love them* instead of giving advice.

If they are clear about what I do for a living, they will know to ask for a coaching session instead of asking for free advice.

And their clarity about this issue is mine to create for them.

Chapter 3

Do it for the love of it all

Hey, Steve, I love the Donald Trump question you ask when someone is stuck in "inaction" and is saying they don't know "what" to do or "how" to do it. (If Donald Trump said he'd give you a million dollars if you got a new client today, how would you do it?)

The thing that struck me, though, is that when I think about getting a client, I immediately feel a sense of desperation or neediness. I am DESPERATE to "close" this client so I can get the million dollars. I NEED to get them to sign or I don't get the million.

I feel like I would throw service out the window in an effort to get that client. Am I exaggerating the exercise or do you see where I'm coming from on this one?

YES this thought experiment can cause BIG TIME mental excitement. But it doesn't have to be a needy type of excitement. It can be a WOW! type of fun game in which you raise your consciousness and awareness SKY HIGH to become super clever and creative.

Years ago, before you were born, a coach I worked with used an even scarier version of this game. He would say to me, "If I put a gun to your head and said I'd shoot you if you didn't get _____ today, what would you do?"

And we would talk from there. Of course, the exercise opened my mind and all kinds of wild ideas flowed out— many of them quite good!

The Donald Trump version I use is a little more gentle. But you can engage the "weaponized" version of this mind game with a client or prospect if they give you permission. It will help them think at a higher level.

And yes, you could still get a client TODAY without being needy or creepy if you really wanted to, and if you pursued it with a singular focus.

And no, you would NOT throw service out the window and try to CLOSE the client, because that would push them away. And you want to get a client, right?

What you would do is INCREASE and INTENSIFY the service. The opposite of throwing it out the window.

Service itself is always the answer.

We just have a hard time seeing it. (At the beginning...)

My favorite Emmet Fox quote applies here and I can promise you that if you want prosperity from your coaching, this would do it for you:

> "If you could only love enough, you would be the most powerful person in the world."
>
> ~ **Emmet Fox**

Chapter 4

Leave the conceptual world behind

The more committed you are to creating a long and strong introductory conversation, the more likely that coaching client prospect will want to work with you.

We are afraid, usually, to do this. **To get to the heart of the matter so early** in the relationship.

It goes against all social conditioning.

We risk looking crazy.

But when we connect, and someone is ready, it's fantastic.

So I recommend that you step up a little bit and make sure those first conversations are huge for the prospect. Not just pleasant, but huge.

Because the short, lighthearted, "Let's get together for coffee and chat" will only have them focused on whether they *like you* and whether they can afford to pay you good money for future fun chats.

Then it's all conceptual rather than experiential.

And selling someone the *concept* of coaching just doesn't work. You want to sell the experience itself.

Chapter 5

Don't be afraid to jump

If there is a fear of falling, the only safety consists in deliberately jumping.

Carl Jung

I have learned to love jumping in.

Where I used to fear it.

And I feared going places only because I was always the one wanting something.

I was the taker, not the giver.

So I feared people would be put off. I was scared I would be rejected as I tried to sell people on my service.

Then I learned to bear gifts. And the gifts were like the wings of an angel... They lifted me up and taught me to soar after that original jump.

Giving happiness to others... Doing things that made them smile and left them better off... Those things are what made jumping fun. Soon I would jump right in, anywhere. Because all I wanted to do was help.

It was no longer about me.

Chapter 6

Take two steps for beginning success

Two steps to success.

Most successful coaching practices follow this pattern:

Find a way to MAKE IT EASY for people to work with you as paid clients.

Once you've done that, and your practice is full up, INCREASE YOUR FEES as a way to manage your time and increase your income.

But wait, you say, *we want to make sure our fees are high enough to sustain our lifestyles!*

Yes. But that comes *after* you are up and running. Many of you are trying to do that *before* you even have a full client list, and it's keeping people from working with you and keeping you from enjoying the coaching process.

If you are a beginner, find a way to MAKE IT EASY for people to work with you so that you are practicing the craft of professional, paid coaching all week long.

Chapter 7

Practice the power of truth

I have a coaching client who keeps missing calls or rescheduling at the last minute. Should I drop her from my world?

Yes, I would drop her. But only after you have a final session in which you compassionately tell her why you are no longer going to work with her.

One of the many wonderful things about coaching (and why it means so much to people) is THE TRUTH.

Most people, in their everyday lives, never hear the truth. They hear evasive, manipulative stories from people in their world.

Tell her the truth: that coaching can only work when she makes an adult commitment to it. Invite her to look at all the other areas in her life where she is cancelling, postponing and rescheduling herself, and to see what impact that has on her relationships and peace of mind.

Maybe the truth will give her a second chance to work with you.

Chapter 8

Be sure to challenge the YES

I have three clients now who said YES to working with me, but who have not sent payments or responded to my emails. What's happening?

You are jumping off the call—and jumping out of the conversation—WAY TOO SOON.

You want to be able to *challenge* their *yes*—not hang up and pop the champagne.

Challenge as in, "Wait a minute. Are you SURE? Do you realize what kind of commitment this will take from you? We may need to talk a bit more about what we've discovered your limiting belief to be."

As for receiving payment, I would let people know how being your client works. So when someone says, "I'm in!" you can say, "Actually, you're not in. Your payment is what puts you in."

We shy away from talk of money and payments at the very moment when they're the best thing to talk about. If someone decides they're in and then doesn't send payment, that's a confidence issue right there. On both sides of the equation, yours and theirs.

THEIR SIDE: "I don't trust myself. I don't trust my initial decision. I said I was in but what is *that* worth? After all it's just *me* speaking."

MY SIDE: I haven't completed the arrangement.

I like to take time talking with a prospect about the difference between *saying* things—like how people say YES to so many things throughout their day and then can't live up to their own promises—and taking *decisive action*, which is what mailing a check represents.

Chapter 9

Don't forget to coach

Your daily activities may be good as you build your practice up, but throughout all this good preparation and contact-making don't forget to coach.

Get a client or a prospect NOW and start coaching, whatever you have to do to accomplish that. Remember that you build a coaching practice by coaching people. No other way to do it. No reason to delay.

Get with people and coach them. Have long, long involved conversations. No one will want coaching because of an email or anything like that. Just as no one gets heart surgery because they get an email from a heart surgeon promoting it.

Enjoy the fact that you are a coach now—and *coach*!

Maybe you'll take some interested person who has "no funds" and coach him for two hours. He'll find the funds. Many of my most lucrative coaching contracts came from people who originally had no funds. Or so they thought. Until their lives were so profoundly changed that they went to their Aunt Millie and borrowed money from her to CONTINUE working with me. Aunt

Millie saw it as an investment in her nephew's education.

It worked for everyone.

Chapter 10

When you have a successful call or visit, DON'T STOP!

Sometimes we get a little success and reward ourselves by stopping.

Then it becomes hard to rekindle the flame later. We lose all the wonderful momentum and enthusiasm.

When you have success, INCREASE your conversations as a response to that success and let prospects hear the LIFE in your happy voice. Enthusiasm makes others enthusiastic.

People want to work with happy people.

Because they want what you've got.

Chapter 11

Learn from the world's best coaches

Becoming a better coach will increase your prosperity.

Like nothing else, in the long run.

Not long ago a coach asked me how she could get better as a coach and I recommended she go to Byron Katie's website (www.byronkatie.com) to read what Katie writes and to watch all her YouTube video clips where she coaches people.

It's always refreshing and edifying to do this, especially if you take your time and really relax into her work. You improve as a coach.

Some people are afraid of Katie's philosophy of loving what is. They worry that it encourages people to just chill out, to stop achieving and be okay with "what is."

Nothing could be further from the truth.

She just knows you have to *start there* to be fully happy and creative.

Keep in mind that Katie is a coach and seminar leader who receives very large fees, as well as an author who receives large book advances from publishers, and she has no trouble making that success fit with her message about how to achieve peaceful freedom using her work.

One of the great misconceptions made about Katie's work is to mistake it for a kind of far eastern passivity where one loves everything—and therefore creates and produces nothing.

Never have I experienced a person who is more in love with her active, energetic work than Katie, or who brings more focus to her career. It's a beautiful thing to see. She creates and produces all day long, and deep into the night. (I attended her nine-day school and watched her in amazement.)

It's just that she doesn't do it to win approval, or because she thinks she "should be doing something with her life." These thoughts never occur to her, because her career is motivated by the joy of serving.

And that's why she's succeeding.

Chapter 12

Stop scaring people away

Some coaches tell me that when they attempt to invite people to have a trial session with them, the people back away and say, "No thanks."

I never want to invite someone into a "session" unless I think they want to have a "session."

But I do want to have lots of *conversations*, and sometimes I'll invite a person to **continue** a conversation when we both have more time. And then we set aside more time.

If the idea of going into a "session" is intimidating to the person you're talking to, just continue the conversation and don't refer to a "session." Use **phrases that relax people,** not phrases that put them on their guard.

For example, you could say, "If you'd like to set some time to brainstorm this a little I have an idea or two that might help. Then again, they may be stupid ideas, but we could have some fun talking."

On the other hand, if someone is talking to you because they know you're a coach, it might be easier to invite them into a session, because that's the context in which they're calling.

The more you converse, the more clients you'll get, so have long conversations with people whether you call them "sessions" or not.

Help people. Serve all day long.

The key is to have *talking to you* be something people love to do, and want to continue doing. So be extremely low key and open at the outset. No ego, no neediness, no personality... Just a beautiful, relaxed LISTENING and a loving curiosity—plus a story or two that gives the person some HOPE.

Chapter 13

Uncover the other person's belief

I know that sales and enrollment are all about the questions I ask. But sometimes I don't quite know what to ask. Can you share a question you ask prospective clients? What's one that's been good for you?

Mine change from week to week. My current favorite question, after a prospect tells me what he or she wants, is:

"Why do you believe this has not happened for you yet?"

Because I believe that people should (and do) already have what they really want, so I want to find out what's behind the illusion that they don't.

What is their limiting and negative belief that keeps them from already having what they say they want?

Good coaching uncovers beliefs. Beliefs are always the only problem. Clients don't always know this, but you do.

That's what makes you so useful to them.

Chapter 14

Stop complexifying your own future

I want to start speaking to groups so I can get clients that way. Any tips?

Hold on a minute.

You have a problem many coaches have. I call it *plural ideation.* (Some of my clients now call it the Clusterf**k but I would never use a word like that, or mention it in a book. Never.)

This plural ideation (CF-ing) stops coaches from getting early traction for building great and prosperous careers.

Your very short question contains two dangerously plural ideas: "groups" and "clients."

The human mind can't handle clusters like that without stress and a sense of prior defeat. It complexifies your future! (I made up that word, too.)

Too many things to think about.

Stress always follows the plural.

Just find ONE place to speak for ONE time and ONE group. Don't go to the overwhelming PLURALs that throw you off and create fear.

When I wanted to be a speaker and seminar leader I just started doing it. I didn't look for plural suggestionS. I'd get *one* suggestion and DO IT. **Just one talk, just one time.**

One group to speak to. One client.

Think that way each day and your whole professional life will take off.

Chapter 15

Focus on the other person's world

I had an intake session with a potential client. I remember asking, "Did you get something from our time together?" Why did I ask that question? I don't really know... It seemed to come from nowhere. I feel like I was being needy. Have you ever done that or known coaches who have? What is the answer to not doing that? In my gut it felt unnecessary to ask.

"Did you get something from our time together?" is a perfectly good question to ask if it comes from a heart-centered desire to HELP another person.

If you are focused on the other person's world, the other person's dissatisfaction with life, the other person's possibility for greater happiness and fulfillment, then you won't worry about what *you* do or say.

Sometimes it helps to drop all self-consciousness.

Drop all sense of coming across as "needy." In fact, stop trying to "come across" altogether. Drop all thoughts of verbal strategy and manipulation and technique.

Instead, help.

Just help another person and do it in a profound way. You won't have any problem loading your calendar with clients if you do that.

Chapter 16

Stop thinking about what they're thinking

Maybe you've left your organization and are now in business on your own as a coach.

Can you reach out to members of your former organization? Of course you can!

Remember that the operative question in a coach's life is: "Would it help?"

Not: "What would they think?"

Coaching careers get better and better the faster we seek to help others and the less we are concerned about what people think of us.

If it were me, I'd send each person a nice message about my previous connection to their company so they could relate to me on that level. I'd tell them why I left and what I was doing. And I'd send along a gift that SERVES THEM RIGHT AWAY. This could be a five-minute Brian Johnson video, an amazing three-paragraph quote, an audio program, an article... Just something they'll benefit from receiving and that's related to personal growth, inspired creativity, energetic spiritual evolution, or whatever lights me and them up. Then I'd invite them to email me back if they're interested in more in-depth material and even a conversation with me.

In other words, send material with accompanying messages like, "Here's something **I would have liked to have known about** when I worked with you at that company…"

Use your own voice and stay focused on the idea of "How can I help these people right away?" instead of "How can I sell them?" or "What would they think if I cold-called them?"

Chapter 17

Stop selling and start serving

The other day I met with an acquaintance from where I used to work. I gave him some advice that he was really grateful for, so I asked about my coaching him. He got really quiet, really fast, like I had said the wrong thing.

You say, "I asked him about coaching."

I would not **ask him** about coaching.

Why not?

I am not a salesperson.

I don't ask people if they want to buy coaching.

I am only here to help.

So instead I ask him about his life.

Then I'll see if there are any other aspects of his life that I can help him with. If there are, I'll start helping him more. The paid coaching conversation can come much later, and *he* can bring it up.

Again, the point here is to *serve*, not to hit people up for coaching.

To serve, and truly serve.

If you do that, they'll hit *you* up.
They'll do the asking.

Chapter 18

Learn to relax another person

When you have a brand new prospect, you have to realize that they're usually scared about the *whole idea* of being coached—not just the money part.

So slow them down. Relax them.

Your first objective is to show them how friendly the atmosphere is, how safe the context is. To give them a very inviting experience so they'll want to continue.

Of course, at times you can challenge them strongly while inside a conversation. When the moment is right, when it serves the client, and when you sense an openness to it on their part.

But early on, your job is research and relaxed bonding.

To learn thoroughly what the client wants to accomplish (and feel) and why it's important and **why it hasn't happened yet.**

The longer the two of you talk, the more your prospect RELAXES about the idea of being coached, because it feels fun and easy and so transformative.

Chapter 19

Improve your conversations

I don't know what's wrong and why so many people are waiting to get back to me and give me an answer about working with me. I am not getting a lot of NOs, but I have a ton of people in limbo. What do you see?

Keep looking at your enrollment process and continuously improve it so it gets stronger and stronger. You always want to be developing an advanced client system, a process that is SO STRONG that no one is ever left promising to call you back. Those kinds of promises are all red flags in the world of coaching.

But they're also opportunities for you to strengthen your systems.

This is the key element of **professional self-esteem**, inner peacefulness and quiet confidence. All good things.

All things that come from **practice.**

When you find you're waiting for people to call *you* with their answer, you are allowing a form of ROLE REVERSAL to seep in. You're giving them all this awesome purchasing power while you're just the supplicant with a beggar's bowl and a sad face.

As if they possess the answer to your prayers.

Don't be pathetic.

This can be very subtle, but if you keep creating ways to BLOW AWAY your prospects by demonstrating what you can do to help them, then they are not going to wait to "get back to you later" about whether they want to work with you. Neither will you allow that suspenseful dynamic to demean you throughout your week. All that waiting by the phone to learn your fate. You don't want that life. And you are subtly creating it. Unknowingly!

So step up. Your path to prosperity is going to come from strength and a better-developed intake process.

Consider the possibility, too, that your prospects are **not seeing enough progress** as a result of talking to you. If they felt that progress they would not "get back to you later" to give you an "answer" while you wait nervously by the phone.

Increase the time spent up front. Show them what you can do. Make it feel crazy for them to go on without you.

This is one of the many beauties of this profession. We always benefit by putting more love and heart into what we do at the very beginning.

Chapter 20

Express your loving curiosity

Can you give me some examples of ways to lead into a conversation with people at a dinner party, as opposed to with someone who is already interested in coaching?

Dinner party: How is life for you these days? What do you have going on? How's your family? What's work like? What kind of challenges are you facing in this economy? Is that the job you always wanted to do?

Someone who's already interested in coaching: What sparked your interest in being coached? What's going on in your world right now? What's the best part of your life? What's *missing* in your life… and how do you keep it out?

In both cases I want to ask questions based on what's already been said in the conversation. So I won't list too many questions here. You want your questions to be driven by intense, in-the-moment curiosity, not by what you've memorized ahead of time. But it's always good to have a few favorite ways to get started.

Chapter 21

Slow down and dive deep

I am really committed to building my practice, and now I'm ready to spend today asking people for referrals. Any suggestions?

Before you ask for referrals, ask yourself:

Why *would* this person refer someone to me?

Just because I've said I'm a coach?

That would never be enough reason. And it's certainly not going to carry a lot of weight with the person they're trying to send to you.

If you tell people you're a coach and would like a referral or two, you've made a very shallow request that's going to land in a very shallow part of the recipient's mind. So even if they pass your name along to someone else, it's going to land in an even shallower part of *that* person's mind.

Welcome to the superficial world of concepts.

Coaching success comes when you leave the world of concepts and enter the wonderful world of *experience*. And, believe me, you'll love it when that happens.

Getting clients is all about two people enjoying the process of going deep with one another.

Please NOTICE that all the trials of shallow sales and marketing techniques we put ourselves through SIMPLY DON'T WORK. (And I mean really *see* this, as opposed to just trying to believe it.)

Is the person doing the referring someone who has a deeply personal experience of how good you are?

If not, forget about asking for referrals and start changing *that* person's life.

Coaching is all about experiences.

Help enough people and you will get referrals without having to ask.

And when you do get a referral? Slow down and prepare to listen openly to your newly-referred prospect, letting the conversational subject matter float deeply into his or her world.

If you really do that, people will *want you to keep coming back into their world.* Don't just try to sell them your generic benefits. Enrollment always takes place in *their* world—not yours.

So get into their world. Keep your focus there.

It's never a numbers game, with you getting lots of referrals and then trying to throw as many proposals as you can out there. It's about how thorough and COMMITTED you are, and how deep you will go with your next prospect.

That's it.

Then when you get your new client, ASTONISH that

client, and you will not have to beg them for referrals. The referrals will come to you unbidden.

I say this from my own experience, and from the experience of the coaches I've worked with who finally learn how to slow down and enjoy their clients.

STEVE CHANDLER ● 51

Chapter 22

Roll up your sleeves and go to work

I'm meeting with a guy tomorrow who says he wants to double his monthly income. What would you do in this situation? How do I get him as a client?

If I wanted him as a client right away I would overwhelm him with my enthusiasm about his life and goals. I would send him Michael Neill's wonderful and funny Ted Talk called "Why Aren't We Awesomer?"

I would then take this guy into a conference room with a white board and do three hours of *drill* with him.

I'd explore this question: "WHY are you NOT earning twice your income NOW?"

I'd ask again and again: "Why aren't you?"

Then: "Why else?" (Make him answer this question at least ten times.)

Then: "If you HAD to double your income WHAT WOULD YOU DO? Let's not leave the conference room until we have put twenty things on the board that you know would lead to doubling!"

(Notice that I'd draw these out of him rather than

provide the answers for him.)

I'd work him and thrill him and exhaust him completely.

He would be on my front porch the next morning with the $$$$$ he'd borrowed from his wife to continue this work with me.

To *continue*.

Not to *start*.

But to *continue*.

Chapter 23

Master the practice of story-telling

Always have your best stories handy, ready to tell.

Stories are so much more powerful than lists of features and benefits. They are even more powerful than lists of testimonials.

I can't tell you how many people have hired me (many) because Steve Hardison has had—at the ready—three or four stories he tells people about me.

Steve is not just the ultimate coach; he is also a master storyteller.

The two are not unrelated.

You can tell stories about how your coaching or consulting created dramatic breakthroughs—in other words CLIENT SUCCESS stories. These go straight to the right side of the prospect's brain, because people *picture* stories and let them in to the part of the brain that gets excited.

Whereas a credentials pitch, a sales pitch about yourself that lists features and benefits and hourly charges—details, details, details—goes immediately to the LEFT BRAIN, which is in charge of sales resistance, budgeting, anxiety, and all the other worrisome activity that leaves a person thinking they probably can't afford you.

Ours is visionary work! Not some detailed, sluggish, hourly-wage thing.

Tell stories.

Someone says "Tell me about your coaching, how does it work?"

You can go into boring detail, or you can tell a story.

Nine coaches out of ten will go hopelessly, impotently, even grotesquely into details: "You get this and that benefit, we can talk this many times a month. You give me your goal list and I review it, and..."

The prospect can NEVER say *yes* to that stuff. They can only go home and think about it.

Why?

The left brain is always worried and careful and flat-out scared. It puts all human monetary activity under the worst-case budgetary microscope.

So here's a different answer to the question, "Tell me about your coaching—how does it work?"

"Well, I just got off the phone with a client who is re-designing her whole business based on what she loves to do versus what she used to think she SHOULD DO. She'd previously burdened herself down with unnecessary staff and marketing campaigns, and when I visited her in Chicago... Well, let me tell you her story...."

Stories sell.

Claims and details do not.

You want your client to hear the story, **picture** the breakthroughs, and feel a surge of excitement that says I WANT A VERSION OF THAT FOR ME!

Chapter 24

Look for problems, not clients

Sometimes an email can work as an initial way to reach out.

But slow down. Take more time than you usually do with the people you're reaching out to by email. And always remember that the goal of the email is to get them on the phone or into your home office.

Rather than have your email be salesy—like right away offering free coaching—you'll want to zero in on a concern of *theirs.*

Have the email be all about them, not you.

Learn more about their particular challenge so that the email is extremely, personally intriguing.

If you can see yourself as a problem-solver instead of a telemarketer you will always look for particular problems. Your intense focus on people's problems will get you clients so fast you won't have time to coach them all.

Most coaches don't do this. They don't focus on helping people solve problems. They focus, instead, on getting clients.

Clients feel that focus! They resist it. Wouldn't you?

If someone says, "I don't have the money to afford you," I just ignore it and say more about their problem. I get them back into the possibility of changing their world so that they can live in it without fear and depression.

Once they get that I am completely focused on their problem and not on my bank account, they find a way to keep talking to me. They can see and feel that I have no real interest in myself right now.

I only care about their problem.

I'm like my doctor!

My doctor says, "How are those headaches?" the very second he sees me on the street.

He never says, "How are the kids?" "How about those Seahawks?" "How's the golf game coming along?"

I love my doctor for that.

Find your prospect's *problem* and get to work on a solution. Otherwise your outreach program will look like the only real problem is that you need clients.

And you can do better than that.

It's so much more fun to be Sherlock Holmes, looking to solve a case, than it is to be a used car salesman.

Chapter 25

Get ready to get real

I have a client who keeps cancelling sessions at the last minute. Do you have anything special you do when that happens?

I know we talked about this earlier, but it's so important I'd like another run at it.

What do I do with a canceler?

I have a ***special conversation*** about only this with my client!

I take the whole hour.

I remind both of us that our sessions are *life* coaching for the evolution of the client's *life*. Not some hassle on the calendar.

When my client chronically cancels for non-emergency reasons they are living in a way that has their own life taking a back seat to pleasing, flattering and impressing other people—a tragically reversed, outside-in, doomed-to-misery approach to the world.

So their cancellation of a session is the cancellation of their own growth in favor of pleasing someone else, someone from whom they think *all their love and sustenance is coming.*

This is not about me and respecting *my* time as a coach. Rather it is a telltale sign that they have no respect for their *own* growth and awakening.

So it's a BIGGER deal than it looks, and I want to USE the cancellation as a major wake-up call for my client.

So we talk about only this habit of outside-in chaos.

We discover where else my client is putting their fear of other people's opinions ahead of their own well-being and growth. We look at why they are scrambling all week long to put the oxygen mask on others while they themselves are running out of life.

I usually only have to have one of these session-long talks, and after that there are no more cancellations with that person.

One of the many great and beautiful things about this profession is that bad things can always be changed into good things. So what looks like a bad thing (client canceling) can turn into a major turnaround session for coach and client.

Chapter 26

Use this code to get clients

There is activity that leads to money and there is activity that does not.

And when you look at your calendar for today, you know which is which.

So you may want to create your day in a way that has you increasing the conversations that lead to money. Am I missing something? Or does this make perfect sense?

This is a CODE you can crack: money talk versus social talk. Money talk is conversation that leads to someone paying you money. Social talk is conversation that does not.

Understanding the simplicity of this code will call forth a QUICKENING for you so that you can round up all the clients you need.

Just allow yourself to create your own day with the same visionary mastery you use to coach other people.

Where are my money conversations today?

If they're not on my calendar, I'm putting them in!

Chapter 27

Stop talking people into coaching

People don't like being talked into things.

They want to feel like they're making up their own minds.

This you probably already know.

I bet you also know that people don't like being talked OUT OF things either.

So how does that good knowledge help you boost your coaching practice?

Here's how: It is often useful and effective to try talking people OUT OF WORKING WITH YOU.

That is, *if you can!!!!* Because, remember, people don't like to be talked out of ANYTHING.

Maybe you'll say something like this: "Are you sure the timing is right for you to take on this coaching project? If it would be better in the future, then it's better that you wait. It'd be a waste of money and time to do this work now if you're not completely ready to change things."

Or this: "As you can see, this represents a lot of money being spent by you. You might want to give yourself a few weeks to think this over and go deep inside yourself to find out if you'll get your money's worth, or whether this will just end up as another of your debts without any return. You'll be the one who determines the return on this investment. If you don't know for sure that you're up for producing a good return, I would definitely not do this work right now."

This is not a literal script, or something to do with everyone. But it *does* illustrate the important point that people DO NOT want to be talked out of anything. So you're far better off trying to talk them out of working with you than into it. Remember that they WON'T WANT to be talked out of working with you.

This kind of conversation would only happen after your prospect has had a very good demonstration of the experience of working with you. And it would happen after they made a tentative or wobbly inquiry about your rates, or spoke a half-hearted desire to work with you.

When people *feel* it... When they really feel the possibility of what working with you could mean for them, your push-back will only *strengthen* their desire and commitment.

And for people who don't feel it yet, and who are only tentatively considering working with you, your push-back earns their respect and restores your own dignity in the relationship. It makes them more likely to want to talk with you further about what the possibilities might be.

And that, as you know, is nothing but good.

Chapter 28

Do what has you helping people now

How important are websites, having a presence on Facebook, blogs, etc., in terms of overall coaching career success and/or giving people a place to go to learn more about you?

In terms of overall success **for coaches**, they are not your top priority.

I'm not saying don't do them. You can. Some coaches do them quite well, and it can help reassure people that you're a professional.

But these activities fall into the category of "fun to work on" once you have your client base and monthly income where you want them to be.

Many coaches notice (after a long year of low income) that they have used all this ancillary activity as a **distraction** from the real mission.

They have been unwilling to see that there's a proven kind of activity that they **already know gets them clients**—and an unproven kind about which they have no clue as to its effectiveness for anything except sucking up their time. Yet they fill their days with it.

We know what our high-return activities are.

We know what our low-return activities are.

And we know what our no-return activities are.

But then we act like we don't know.

And we start to panic about things we never needed to panic about in the first place, mostly out of a habit of living a scary life from panic to panic. Like trying to cross a rushing stream on slippery stones, we go from one internet panic to the next.

True enrollment is the activity that's going to get you the client base that creates the monthly income you want. So your ONLY problem in all of this will be the problem of distraction. From what you *know* to do!

This is all very good news, by the way, because it frees you up from your former life of internet confusion: Personal branding? A niche? A presence? Marketing?

Much easier to cut to the chase.

Much easier to just go get a client *today*.

Chapter 29

Pump more time and love into it

What if you talk to some guy for ninety minutes, have a great conversation, and leave with the person saying they "think" they want to work with you. They say they'll "decide" in a day or two.

And then they never call back.

What is going on? What can you learn from this?

How about this: Ninety minutes was not enough.

Because if he REALLY wanted coaching with you, you'd be coaching him now. So in fact he SORT OF, kinda wanted it.

He liked talking to you, for sure! But so what? You're building a practice, not a fan club.

If I want a person to be my client, I always make sure they REALLY (and I mean *really*) want to work with me before I offer them anything at all.

Your option in this case is to reconnect and create a relationship and a profound experience for this guy that makes working with you something he wants enough to PAY FOR and BOOK HIS FIRST SESSION NOW.

As in right now. Right this very minute. While you are

still talking to him.

Your clue that he was not ALL IN was that he still had to "decide." He told you he would **decide** in the future. That means that you were way too premature in offering him coaching.

Imagine asking someone out, and her saying she'll decide in a week or two whether she'll go out with you.

She's just not into you.

Chapter 30

Stop worrying about your value

Many of us, particularly at the start of our careers, waste a lot of time worrying about our value.

Notice this about questioning our own value: We don't ever have to question our value if we are willing to make a difference.

Value is something we will find together. You'll let me know if you want to keep talking to me based on whatever experience we have talking together.

If someone I just met asks me, "Would your coaching be valuable for me?" My answer is, "How the heck would I know? Let's try it out! You might not be COACHABLE!!!!"

I'd want to find that out before I agreed to work with anyone.

Low professional self-esteem will take care of itself. The more people you coach, the higher your self-esteem and confidence will get! But for NOW, just get into action and help someone.

Just make a difference in someone's life.

Chapter 31

Help them transcend the hidden fear

Most potential clients don't really know what coaching is.

We assume they do, because we think about coaching all day long. But they don't. And they certainly don't know what coaching with *you* would be like.

Maybe they've been coached by someone else (that's usually rare, but it happens) so maybe they think that's what coaching is and that it doesn't work.

Or maybe they think coaching is something they've seen on TV, with Tony Robbins confronting someone during an intervention or Dr. Phil getting in someone's face. Or they've had some psychotherapy.

So they have some vaguely frightening idea about coaching.

Once you really get into a deep conversation with a prospect, you often find that they have a lot of fear around coaching, but it isn't the fear you think it is.

You as the coach think the prospect has fear about whether you have the right credentials, credibility, résumé, reputation, ability, intelligence, background, and so on.

But that's not what the fear is.

The *actual* fear for the prospect is that they will not do *their* part correctly, that they won't get it right—they won't know *how* to **be coached**.

She doesn't know if she *knows* how to share herself.

He doesn't know how much he should say.

And there's an additional fear—she doesn't know how you will *judge her* if she's really honest about why she's not living a great life right now. She doesn't know how she'll be seen by you. The more you try to impress her with how credentialed you are, the more she feels your superiority, the less she wants to open up. She doesn't know what you'll think of her.

So she is understandably reluctant to enter into this relationship.

She eventually uses money as her reason to say no. But this isn't the reason.

Most coaches I work with (before they spend time in the Coaching Prosperity School) have no idea that these are the prospect's fears! So they just forge ahead and go on about how good a coach they are, crowing about "my credibility, my expertise, here's who I've coached before, here's why you'll want me, here's how you'll pay me, here's how many hours you'll get!"

And all the while the prospect is sitting on this fear and uncertainty and feeling of inadequacy; nothing's being done to alleviate it. She's left thinking, "I don't know if I can do this. I don't know if I'll be any good at it."

There's a way to solve this, and it's called listening. And asking gentle questions. And creating a relaxing and rewarding experience for the client.

It's called giving them a chance to be good at it.

Chapter 32

Don't be afraid of a spouse

I really admire the coaches I've coached who include their client's spouse in the enrollment process.

Most coaches never do that.

Never!

They bite their nails and fret when the prospect says, "My spouse is worried. I'll get back to you." And then the prospect never gets back. The coach never completes the relationship.

The fear of spouse factor!

But great client enrollment occurs when there is no fear, when we welcome **every** development inside each conversation, and all news is good news.

That's when we are being creative. And compassionate. If the prospect mentions a spouse, that's just another paint on our palette! Bring her in. Let's all three meet for a good, long meeting.

Sometimes when I've done that, both people end up being my clients. How good is that?

No fear.

Chapter 33

Just have that one talk today

Is the answer just to have more and more conversations with people? Because none of the other things I'm trying seem to work.

You ask if the answer is to have "more conversations with people," but that can never happen.

I'll say this again. You can only have a conversation with one person—your next person.

So really have your day be about your next person.

I'll return to my word "complexify" again: Every time we generalize and make things big and sweeping and overwhelming and intimidating, our minds get scared and shut down. But when we reach out and connect with one person, the mind relaxes and gets creative.

Someone once asked my coach, the ultimate coach, Steve Hardison, how many clients he had.

He said, "One. The one I'm with."

Chapter 34

Don't make this a horror movie

I did a free talk to a group of people last year and got all their contact info from a form I passed around. They loved the talk, but now I'm wondering, how do I reconnect with them?

We seem to be hitting on the same theme here. (We do things once for information, twice for transformation.)

And I'll keep stressing this as many times as I have to for you to see the light and learn and prosper.

You need to slow down.

You need to find ONE person out of that group and ask yourself "How do I reconnect with her?"

Or him.

Not THEM.

There's a horror movie out there called *THEM.*

You might want to watch it! In the movie we see that the earliest atomic tests in New Mexico have caused common ants to mutate into giant, man-eating monsters that threaten civilization.

Instructive!

Take your list. Once you've connected with just one person, slowly and creatively, then very, very deliberately pull—careful now—another name from the list, the second-best name. Ask yourself, "How do I reconnect with HER?" Be clever and service-minded about it.

When rushing about, we tend to try getting into our own future, like a fly tries to get into my house by flying straight into the window glass. Ouch. Over and over. Bang, bang!

When we're thinking this fast, we tend to think in **clusters**.

We think of "groups" and "people" instead of waking up to the intimacy of our real work.

It's about *one* person. That's all it ever is.

Chapter 35

Stop impressing your friends

Sometimes we put our "dear friends" ahead of ourselves and our own wealth and health and well-being.

Because we believe they are so vital to our personal sense of being approved of in this world.

We do all kinds of things to "help" (which usually means "impress") them and secure the "relationship." For our own emotional security.

Then one day we wake up and realize that what we are "giving" many of them is our own limited, precious, professional service.

Would a doctor do brain surgery, maybe remove a tumor, to help a dear friend with migraines? Would a construction worker go to a friend's house and build him a deck and a porch over two weeks' time, ignoring himself and his own business in the process?

No, because they know the difference between friendship and business.

Look for instances where your own "dear friend" story is another way to avoid embracing the scary truth: You are a powerful professional who deserves to be paid for

EVERY LAST BIT of your work.

It may be scary for a while, but soon your friends will begin respecting you more and more.

Chapter 36

Make your fee sound good to *you*

Stop trying to figure out what a "fair price" would be for your coaching.

Make up a *good* price.

Say it out loud.

Now make up a lesser price. Say that one. Now make up an even larger price than the first one. Say it.

You will know your price. It will resonate and harmonize with *where you are* in the evolution of your career. Which is to say, in your heart and in your own ears.

And then take "fair" out of the thought process.

It isn't a fair or unfair price. It could only be unfair if you were going to go *seize* the money against your client's will. That would be unfair. But if they have free will, and can choose to pay it or not, then the price can never be "unfair."

A better question might be, "What's a FUN price to charge?"

If someone says my fee is more than they expected, I say, "I would hope so. I do NOT want this to be an easy decision for you. I want this to be a major commitment. My fee serves to filter out the uncommitted."

Last year I had a person call me to say he wanted to be my apprentice. When he heard it would take $X0,000 to work with me for a year he nearly fainted. I was so happy. I quickly told him, "Wait. It gets worse. Not only do you pay all that absolutely unaffordable money, but then you have to travel all over for a year at your own expense to learn all my seminars and work harder than you've ever worked to learn my content and challenging sales techniques. By the time you reach your tenth month of work with me you'll wish it was over."

How's that for a slick come-on? The more we value the work we do the more we will WANT to challenge prospects with our strong fees to weed out the uncommitted and people with no real, serious ambition. My apprentices have been extremely committed and they have succeeded big-time after the apprenticeship.

It might seem that strong fees for our high-end programs would reduce our earning power, but they only increase it.

When someone babysits, they charge per hour because you're paying for the hour they spend watching your kid. That's it.

When people pay a coach like you they pay for everything you've ever done—not to mention all the books you've read, the seminars you've attended and all the other work you do (including BEING coached in profound ways) to make yourself the best coach you can be. That's what you'll be bringing to the table...

A woman once saw Picasso doodle on a napkin in a

restaurant. She went over to his table and asked him how much she'd have to pay to have the napkin.

He said, "$20,000."

She said, "What?!? I watched you, and it only took you five minutes to do it!"

He said, "True... But it took me thirty years to *be able* to do it."

Chapter 37

Keep it simple, keep it clean

Out of clutter, find simplicity.

Albert Einstein

This short, five-word life instruction from Einstein actually contradicts our common picture of him.

We picture Einstein as a complex genius.

We picture myriads of bridges and power stations running through his multifaceted mind. We define that as genius.

So we seek our own version of genius.

And rather than do what Einstein actually *did*—find simplicity out of clutter—we always try to be *more* complex.

We add things.

We think geniuses thrive on complexity and additional tools, so we add complexity and tools to our own lives.

New books. New websites. New "friends." New systems. New pretty things. New apps. New hobbies. New infatuations. New shoes… And the clutter mounts.

Soon the borders of hoarding are reached. Unfortunately there is no fence and there are no guards.

And yet, all the while, the power was in simplicity.

So. Keep it simple. Keep it clean. **And at the start of every week do something really bold to simplify your life even further.**

I only say this because the people I coach who do this become more successful. And when I do this myself, the same thing happens. Now it's your turn.

Remember that progress comes from trying these tips, not from agreeing with or believing in them.

You can make your life less conceptual and more experiential every day!

The trouble is, you think you have time.

~ Buddha

Part Two

The 17 Lies Coaches Tell Themselves

(until they wake up)

Introduction

Truth is the most *advanced* *client system* of all

I agree that LIE is too harsh a word.

I'm using it just to get your attention.

Shock value.

These are more like self-deceiving beliefs, a little different from outright lies, I admit. But let's not split hairs. They match up perfectly with those in my *17 Lies That Are Holding You Back* book. An eerie coincidence... but, of course, not really.

The ultimate self-deception, and really the biggest problem coaches have, is believing they are not running a business. They are not a part of free enterprise, participating in the global marketplace. That problem often causes them to not do well financially.

So let's get over that one.

All I need is a sheet of paper and something to write with, and I can turn the world upside down.

~ Friedrich Nietzsche

Lie #1

It's who you know

Everyone walks around saying, "It's who you know."

That's their opinion. That's their analysis!

If you know somebody in a position of power over in that business, in that family… If you know somebody who knows somebody, then you're luckier and can sell faster than other coaches.

It's all about your connections. It's all about your contacts.

But great coaching careers are not that shallow. They're not built on precarious cynicism. This is not a house of cards.

Sure, to a certain degree it *is* valuable to know people in the community, or to know a lot of people in a certain business, but that only gives you a small head start.

It's not the whole picture. It's not even very important. And it's certainly not the end-all.

But that's how people try to portray it.

In the end, it's *not* who you know—that's not the most important thing. In the end the most important thing is **what you can do.**

If you can help me, do I really need to "know" you, or know whether you went to Harvard Business School, or know if your father knows my father?

People who enroll clients successfully don't need to be shallow publicity seekers. They drop all their worry about status and credentials and instead start to get close to their prospects.

They get right into the coaching.

There are secrets to our world that only practice can reveal, and no opinion or analysis will ever capture in full.

~ Nassim Nicholas Taleb

Lie #2

There's something wrong with me

When people are failing in what they're doing, whether it's wealth creation or something else, you'll always hear them say:

"I've got some kind of personal problem. There's something about me that's a weakness, or something about my character or my makeup that isn't strong, that doesn't allow me to succeed to the same degree that other people succeed."

This is simply not true.

There is nothing "wrong" with you. I have never sat across from a coach who had anything wrong with them.

Yet it's a very popular thing to say. "There's something wrong with me!"

It's a very common thing. A craze, almost. With some coaches I work with it's their main focus in life. They wake up into it. The story of their patterns, habits, and profound weaknesses of character and personality. They create a personal soap opera for the ego to work through. They become hypnotized by their own issues.

But are these defects even true?

They do make for a good story. Let's say *your* history (notice I'm not saying personality, trait or anything that suggests permanence) is that of what you would call in high school a "nerd" or brainiac type—an introvert, someone who is shyer and more of a hesitant, laid-back communicator.

Well, that very history is something that can be *used* to inspire great warmth and trust in clients and prospects. There isn't any history you feel is a weakness that cannot be used as a genuine strength.

And none of it is permanent!

The way your past pattern can be converted into a strength is for you to **not focus on yourself**. To not obsess about your so-called weakness, but to focus on the client.

The key to freedom from a fixed, imprisoned "personality" is to continue to turn your attention away from "you" and zero in on *actions*. Instead of always looking at yourself, look for ways to serve the client. You can replace self-centeredness with curiosity about the other person's life:

"How can I help you? What's your life like? Who are your customers? What are *they* like? What are your greatest dreams? What are your greatest fears?"

The more I focus on the client, the less my imaginary "shortcomings" affect me, and when they do come through, they come through as experiences I can draw upon to demonstrate empathy and compassion. I can say I've been there.

If I don't manage to fly someone else will.
Spirit wants only that there be flying.

~ Rainer Maria Rilke

Lie #3

I'm too old for that

Many people walk around saying, "I'm too old for this, I'm too old for that, I'm too old to get *enthusiastic* about selling. I'm too old to get excited, to get fired up, to really go gung-ho. I'm too old to learn a new profession."

Then, after a failed day of attempted selling they continue to groove on it: "I'm too old to exercise, I'm too old to get really healthy and in good shape, I'm too old to be really romantic..."

I once had a person come up to me in a seminar who was about thirty-five years old and she said, "You know, I've always wanted to be an actress. That was my dream, that was my goal, all my life, even as a little girl. Of course, now I'm too old for that."

I said, "What do you mean?"

She said, "Well, to be an actress, to really do it right, you have to start when you're young. You have to start as a teenager and go to acting school. You have to do touring and off-Broadway and things like that, and you have to really build a foundation. By the time you're thirty-five, like me..."

And I said, "Oh, I see. Okay, but maybe your

limitation is in your own mind!"

She stared at me like I was criticizing her.

Her expression told me she was thinking, "How dare you criticize me? That's *my* job!"

But I wasn't criticizing her.

It's just that when a person is chronically self-limiting, they have huge sensitivity to external criticism, and will take a potentially helpful comment to be a wounding judgment of them.

One of the things I wanted to say to this person but didn't think of until later (you know how you always think of things later that would have been wonderful to say at the time?) is that the actor John Houseman would be worth learning about. He started acting when he was seventy-one years old. Seventy-one! And then he won an Academy Award! So he actually became quite a good actor. Seventy-one was not too old for that.

So she's not too old for that. That's a lie.

Younger people use a customized version of this lie when they say, "I'm too *young* for that!"

They say, "I'm too inexperienced. I don't have any credibility with these clients. They've been in the world for so many years and they know it inside-out. How are they going to trust me? If I'm going to be an advisor to this person, how are they going to trust me and listen to me?"

Well, really, you are *not* too young for that, because if your position is "I am going to serve you, I am going to take great care of you, I admire you and respect you," being young fits into that picture quite nicely. Because the focus is on the client and not on you or your age.

Drop these false fears so you can learn to fly!

The moment that you feel that, just possibly, you're walking down the street naked, exposing too much of your heart and your mind and what exists on the inside, showing too much of yourself. That's the moment you may be starting to get it right.

~ Neil Gaiman
University of the Arts Commencement Speech

Lie #4

I can't because I'm afraid

This is the lie that grown-ups tell that children don't tell.

It especially hits people in the world of business. (Which coaches are, but usually wish they weren't—until they learn to love and master the practice of growing their business.)

Grown-ups, unlike children, equate being *afraid* to do something with not being *able* to do it.

They equate being nervous about doing something with complete lack of ability. They believe that being intimidated by someone prevents them from having a conversation.

Let's look at how this fear, based on false fantasies about the future, keeps me in poverty.

Let's say I'm afraid to ask someone for time to talk. A chance to demonstrate my coaching.

I'm having a nice conversation, everything is going well, I can tell that my prospect likes the experience and I know that right now is probably a good point to ask that person to set aside some extra time for a deeper exploration of their problem. So I say to myself, "Should

I ask? Should I ask for the time? Should I just very naturally say, 'May I work with you on this?'"

But I don't say anything. I don't say a word. I just keep listening and making friendly small talk.

Why?

When I look back I tell myself, "It was because I was afraid. I couldn't do it because I was afraid to."

Cause and effect, right? Being afraid means being incapable. They are the same, right?

Not right!

Let's look clearly at this "I-can't-because-I'm-afraid" belief. Children don't buy into it. Children quite often are afraid but also do the very thing they are afraid to do. For the thrill.

They only learn *later* in life to duck out of everything they're afraid of—that becomes their new practice, but only later on.

When they're young they do all kinds of things they're afraid of. They get up on bikes they're afraid to get up on, they get up on a high dive and jump off, even though they're afraid. They try all kinds of scary things.

As they get older they talk themselves into a personality, an identity that carries with it permanent, pervasive fears. And not just small fears, but disabling, disempowering fears. That's the adult story of life and its limitations.

Simply lies.

One of the greatest things we can do as coaches is say, "Hey, I'm afraid to do this, but I'm going to do it anyway. I'm intimidated by this person, but I'm going to call him anyway. This scares me, and I'm going to do it."

Once committed, once I know I'm doing it, I can now go to the second level of self-inquiry: **How can I make this fun for me?** Now that I'm just going to DO IT.

Because if I can start doing that, it is thrilling… This life of coaching becomes pure adventure. It is so exciting to do the things I thought I was afraid to do!!!

If I'm afraid to call someone, if I'm afraid to do anything, the best thing I can do for my enrollment and hitting my goals, for my own prosperity, for my family and my self-esteem, is to **do it anyway**. To break the cause-and-effect chain. Break it again and again. So that being afraid and **not doing it** are no longer joined at the hip. They are no longer locked in mutual causation.

Once I learn how easy it is to break this chain, I can start working on it with my clients. Do they have this chain? Well, only all of them.

A lot of my clients say, "I didn't remember that part of my childhood until we started doing that together— breaking that chain."

One of the first things I like to do with the coaches I coach is to help them break the chain. Soon they're helping their own clients break this sinister chain that binds all adults to their fears.

In the now-famous words of Ambrose Redmoon, "Courage is not the absence of fear, but rather the judgment that something else is more important than fear."

If being hard on yourself was going to work,
it would have worked by now.

~ Jamie Smart

Lie #5

What doesn't kill me makes me stronger

What doesn't kill me makes me stronger.

Really?

This lie has everything to do with self-destruction.

It's a lie about addictions we pretend not to have (and I've talked in my previous books about my addictions).

Before I received the gift of a recovery program and a sponsor (my first real coach!), I had many addictions. But my primary addiction was alcohol.

(It was the perfect addiction for my victim mindset: "Poor me, poor me, pour me another.")

For years I was in denial. It was destroying my life and I was saying things like, "Well, you know, what doesn't kill me makes me stronger!"

Anything that's physically and mentally self-destructive can't be making me stronger. It can't even be giving me relief from anything. And the minute I woke up to that and saw my way to a new clarity, my life got good.

We can't coach people who have an active addiction to drugs or alcohol unless the coaching is focused 100% on getting them help for the addiction. Why? Because the coaching won't land anywhere that's clean or clear inside that person. It will land on top of the addiction and the "stinking thinking" that negates all wisdom in favor of finding the next fix or drink.

We're better off releasing the coaching client until the client can achieve some good clean and sober time. I know about this. I *was* that addicted person. No amount of wisdom or guidance got through to me while I was still drinking. (Although many good people tried. I broke their hearts.)

The irony for me is that I finally was made stronger. But it wasn't the wild times and the drinking that did it. It was the recovery. And my willingness to surrender my ego to the guidance of a wise and compassionate sponsor who coached me back into clarity and joy.

You have to build systems
to protect against your lesser self.

~ Neil Strauss

Lie #6

There's nothing I can do

Notice how all of these lies are lies you tell to keep yourself out of action. These lies blind you from seeing your next creative act.

But you don't have to believe them anymore. Each one of these lies is corrected by the adoption of a new **system designed for action**.

Let's look at objections.

Someone you want as a client will have an objection. They'll say, "No, I can't meet with you. I'd love to be coached but I don't have time to commit to it right now. See me in five months. See me a year from now. See me two years from now."

And you think, "Oh wow, **there's nothing I can do.** They don't want to talk to me."

Well, wait a minute here. What do you mean there's nothing you can do? That's not true.

Even though they might think they don't want to talk to you now, and they don't want to give up a lot of time, they don't want to listen to all your sales pitches, because they've told you that, it doesn't follow that **there's**

nothing you can do.

Maybe they would appreciate a book and a handwritten note from you with a new idea about how you could begin the work and what it would accomplish. Maybe a new idea about how you could assist them in another way that wouldn't take any time to communicate.

An objection is just a client telling me how things *can* work. When he says it *can't* work because of Obstacle A, he is also saying, "It *could* work if you can find the answer to Obstacle A."

Sometimes I like interpreting someone's "no" to really mean, "Can't you be more creative than that?"

It's not true when I say **there's nothing I can do.** There's always something I can do.

We always have more choices in life than we realize.

Many, many more.

If an egg is broken by outside force, Life ends. If broken by inside force, Life begins. Great things always begin from inside.

~ Jim Kwik

Lie #7

I worry because I care

People say, "I worry about my future because I care. I worry about the business because I care. I worry about my daughter because I care. I worry about my wife because I care. I worry about my husband's drinking because I care so much."

That's not true.

I may indeed care. And I may worry. But I don't worry *because* I care. The truth is, I worry because I worry.

I worry because I worry because I worry.

People worry because they are in the habit of worrying. Their worrying is not the same as converting *genuine concern into action*—that's a different experience altogether!

Worry is a default to the wheel-spinning, pointless, unproductive cul-de-sac of mindless overthinking.

The reason you worry is because you have gotten in the habit of worrying. In some funny way, it gives you a sense that you are paying some sort of attention to the problem. You're at least not ignoring the problem! After all, you *are* worrying about it!

Is that how you want to address problems?

Because worry is actually a misuse of the imagination.

It's like using your iPad to drive a nail into wood.

It's a dysfunctional misuse of the right side of the brain. And it is not caused by caring. (If I REALLY cared, I'd be in action.)

So how do I quit worrying? What do I replace it with?

The most effective approach to anything that worries me as a coach is to ask a quick question. If something bothers me in any way, if it concerns me and I catch myself about to open a fresh can of worrying, then I want to immediately ask this quick question:

What can I do about this right now?

What action can I take?

What needs to be done?

If there is no action whatsoever that I can conceive of taking after brainstorming it with myself, then there's no reason to worry about it.

If there's no solution, there's no problem.

It's now just a fact of life, it's part of the playing field.

So let's get going.

Let's get back into this wonderful game.

Opportunity: it's not really scarce.
It's everywhere.
If you really were any good,
you'd be overwhelmed by it.

~ **Werner Erhard**

Lie #8

I'm sadder now, but wiser

If you were really any good, you'd be overwhelmed by opportunity.

Some people think this is a sad thing to hear.

But you can also hear it as a very happy truth. Because it reminds you that opportunity is not in the hands, or at the whim, of other people. Opportunity is yours to create. So now you are back to doing all the things that make you good at what you do.

Instead of indulging sadness.

"I'm sadder now, but wiser" is often the ultimate lie of someone who has given up on their coaching career.

I'm just going to give up. There's no opportunity.

I'm going to slowly quit.

I'm going to approach everything with low energy from now on.

You can see how sadness is just a form of low energy. It is not a result of a clear evaluation of anything.

It's simply not true that wisdom and sadness go together.

The truth is, when I am *truly* wiser, I am happier.

If I'm learning more and more and more about how this entrepreneurial coaching life works, how sales works, how free enterprise works, how psychology works, how my clients think, how my clients dream, how the mind works, what spirit really is, then I am becoming *truly* wiser. And the more of this I get, *the happier I am.*

So when people try to persuade other people in their profession or their company or their families that, "If you knew as much as I knew, you'd be kind of melancholy too. I'm sadder now, but wiser," now you know that's just an absolute lie; don't buy that from anybody.

Especially from yourself.

If you hear a voice within you say "you cannot paint," then by all means paint, and that voice will be silenced.

~ **Vincent van Gogh**

Lie #9

The longer I have a habit, the harder it is to break

This is a very interesting lie, because almost everybody believes it.

I believed it for most of my life.

I kept bad habits I didn't have to keep because of this belief.

(I've come to see that the only problem anyone ever has is believing things that are not true.)

When my first few clients tried to sell me on this lie, I would always buy their stories.

You've had this habit of procrastination all your life? Oh, okay! Now I understand why it would be so hard to break that one. You've had the habit a *long time*!

Then something changed for me.

I started doing some work with a hypnotherapist by the name of Lindsay Brady. He became one of my best friends (and he is a very fascinating, brilliant man). One of the things he taught me when I first got to know him was that a habit, once it gets into the system, is no harder to break if you've had it for thirty years than if you've had it for one month.

Say what?

Lindsay Brady has successfully helped a lot with people who wanted to quit smoking. His experience is that if he gets a smoker in his office who has been smoking for, say, sixty years (someone seventy-five years old who started smoking at the age of fifteen), that person will go through *exactly the same process* in quitting smoking as someone who has been smoking for one year—some nineteen-year old who started at eighteen.

They will go through the same process! And they will take the same amount of time to quit!

So it's not really true that the longer you have a habit the harder it is to break.

The truth is, any habits can be quickly replaced once your commitment to do so is crystal clear. Especially if you don't re-visit your decision every other moment.

And step number two, after the choice is made, is to always *replace* that habit with a new one that is better for you than the old habit.

So the habit of seeing myself as a smoker is replaced by seeing myself as someone with healthy lungs who enjoys breathing fresh air. Someone whose lungs grow stronger every day.

If my habit is one of being an alcoholic drinker, I can replace that false pursuit of spirit with a true program of spiritual recovery. Replacement! No matter how long the habit was there, I can always replace it.

The more you know, the less you need.

~ Yvon Choinard

Lie #10

People really upset me

Anyone who says that people upset them is disconnected from reality.

If I think this person upsets me, management upsets me, the receptionist upsets me, my client upsets me, my wife upsets me—I am exhibiting a fundamental misunderstanding of how the human brain (a teachable, learnable bio-computer!) works.

Yes, the brain works in better ways than we know. Why would it not? Why would the brain be a mere receiver of upset from others? Our brain is here to serve us, not upset us.

The first step in restoring my brain to its original intended use (as a creator of my reality) is understanding this: The only thing in life that can upset me is my own judgment of something.

My brain's story about a situation is what upsets me. Not the situation.

If I get a call saying, "Steve, we've decided not to have you come in and coach our people," I can attach *any story I want* to that communication.

My favorite is, "I've been spared!"

I like that story because it has me happy enough to keep enjoying my day and creating new clients.

Or: I can choose, out of habit, to get that news and then see myself as a failure whose practice is not going anywhere.

But why not *enjoy* the hunt? Why not create a world in which there is no such thing as rejection? It's all just good information.

I could see a "no" as an upsetting setback. That's one choice. But I can also choose to see it as information that could help me succeed. That's my choice, too. Some of the best sessions I've had coaching other coaches were the ones in which we studied the process that led up to the "no." We learn so much. We see so many alternative possibilities for the future! And without that "no" we wouldn't have had that great session. And without that great session, there would not have been the quantum leap in growth.

I can think the person who decided not to return my calls and emails has upset me, but if I do so I am not being accurate. No one can upset me. No one has that power. Only *my* thoughts can upset me.

Or lift me up.

It all occurs at the level of story. It's invented. Inside me. It never occurs out there where I think it's occurring. Once I fully understand this, I can change how anything is now occurring to me.

By the way, neither one of those choices ("upsetting" or "uplifting") is the absolute truth. They are simply optional stories!

If I have an option, why not exercise my option?

* * *

Now here's a confession for you: I didn't immediately take to this profession of coaching.

In my darker days, I used to hate my job. Too many of my clients at that time were blaming other people for their suffering. Ex-husbands were evildoers and business partners didn't trust each other.

Clients were telling me about how someone had really "triggered" them, and it was taking days to get over it.

Back then I was not doing what I would do today.

Today I would help that person see the triggering for what it was. Their own story. And it wouldn't be long before we'd get on with their life, and all its possibility. (We would melt the trigger down to liquid, pour it into a mold and make a nice ring out of it. Not necessarily a wedding ring—but at least a friendship ring.)

But in the early days I didn't know how to do that. So I just got grumpier when clients pointed the finger. I even fantasized at one point that it might be profitable to simply become a Revenge Coach. Helping people get back at others. (In subtle ways, of course.)

But fortunately that internal cloud passed and I began to see that I was doing exactly what my clients were doing. I was pointing my finger at them and claiming that they were "triggering" me!

Lovely that this profession requires growth.

This is the manner of noble souls: they do not want to have anything for nothing; least of all, life. Whoever is of the mob wants to live for nothing; we others, however, to whom life gave itself, we always think about what we **might best give in return...** One should not wish to enjoy where one does not give joy.

~ Friedrich Nietzsche

Lie #11

Winning the lottery would solve everything

I once had a mentor who studied suicide.

He was a very knowledgeable person and his focus in life was suicide. That was his expertise. He helped a lot of people and families and prevented many suicides. When he was at graduate school in college, his focus was the linguistics of suicide.

One of the things that he noticed while studying suicide was that it taught him a lot about human happiness. Suicide's opposite. (For this whole thought thing exists on a continuum, does it not?) And he discovered that such happiness was never produced by anything external to the human being.

Like winning the lottery.

It was always an inner sense of peace that produced it. Or an even smaller, sweeter sense of usefulness.

So winning the lottery, or any other unearned money that comes in a windfall to someone, does not solve anything.

In fact, it usually causes fresh, new, unexpected

trouble!

Studies of lottery winners show that people who win the lottery (seven people out of ten in a recent study) wish they had never won less than five years later.

Why? Well, windfall money was exciting for a while, but then their lives became nightmarish. The money went away, they made bad investments, relatives hit on them constantly, some finally had to move, some of them even changed their names because they couldn't go through an hour without some relative or friend calling and saying, "Hey, you know you didn't really *earn* that money, why don't you give us some of it? I've got a daughter who is really sick and you just won it in the lottery. You going to keep it? You going to buy a boat with it? How's that fair?"

Unearned money is spent and invested differently than earned money. It is not respected, it's not considered my life's energy, it's just considered to be a lucky bonus. So it's not really true that winning the lottery would solve everything.

Because it's not the money you make that solves your money problems.

It's the **money-making strength** you build inside yourself that solves your money problems.

It's your creatively-developed resourcefulness that solves your problems.

Not the money itself.

Coaching is an especially good profession for learning this.

Because most other professions have fairly fixed

incomes. Or they have incomes dependent on other people evaluating and paying you based on bureaucratic timetables. Or promotions based on your skill at office politics.

Soon, you lose your connection to yourself. You curry favor. You seek approval all day.

Whereas a person offering coaching services develops the mastery of her own actions, her own energy, her own detective work, her own willingness to learn and understand clients. Her practice of joy-giving. Soon her own willingness to inspire a breakthrough in someone else's life produces a wonderful feeling about a new way to enroll somebody, a new way to connect and create.

These are the things that make people feel great about themselves. Money that comes from doing these kinds of activities feels wonderful. Because what you are feeling is not the money itself, but rather your inner resourcefulness. The skillful way you've learned to make a difference.

When you have exhausted all possibilities, remember this—you haven't.

~ Thomas Edison

Lie #12

They're too beautiful for this world

This lie is what I tell myself when I'm thinking I personally don't fit the world marketplace or the free-enterprise system.

Thinking I'm too innocent, too soulful, too honest, to be good at earning money. Too close to the earth. Too real. Too compassionate, and too caring. Too angelic. Too authentic. Too spiritual!

Often we think this of ourselves: "I have to be a con man to become rich and I'm not willing to be a con man. I have to be kind of a huckster, and I'm not willing to do that. I'm too honest, I'm too pure and straightforward to learn to make money."

The truth of the matter is, this is simply a lie.

Every time I went into a client's organization or school to train and coach a team of salespeople or fundraisers I found out about this lie.

When I got to meet the people who were doing well, people who were breaking records and creating prosperity for themselves, I found that *they* were the people who really were good, compassionate people.

They weren't people who were scammers, shallow hucksters, and con men and women.

They were the more principled people who worked with integrity and authentic service as their mission.

It was the cynical ones who kept trying to *manipulate* people into buying who had the hardest time succeeding. And people who believed they were too beautiful to sell anything are the ones who were the most manipulative and phony with others when they did try to sell! Ironic. Beyond ironic... Hilarious!

The successful ones were *more* vulnerable and genuine. They were people who took a real interest in their clients. They were the people who succeeded the fastest.

The coaches I know who realize they are serving another person's life succeed fast because they know that *selling* is the only way people can get the coaching. It has to be contracted first! And that's actually strong and good! (Not a crying shame, as the beautiful people believe.)

People who master a generous and service-oriented coaching practice care deeply about other people and, therefore, find possibilities for business everywhere!

There will come a time when you believe
that everything is finished. That
will be the beginning.

~ **Louis L'Amour**

Lie #13

You hurt my self-esteem

People often think their professional self-esteem depends upon whether they are respected and treated well by others.

They have a misconception of what self-esteem is.

There is a clue to where self-esteem comes from in the word "self-esteem."

Notice that it's called **self**-esteem. It's not called others-esteem. It's called self-esteem.

It's what I think of myself based on my own behavior, my own responses to other people, my own creativity, my own service, my own success. It also comes from having enough of a spiritual practice (prayer, meditation, spiritual study) to relax about outside approval and actually *feel* a connection, an inner link to the universal good.

If you can help your clients start to see this the right way, they will want to work with you for a long time.

The reward for conformity is that everyone likes you but yourself.

~ **Rita Mae Brown**

Lie #14

It's a shame we didn't capture that on video

People who focus excessively on the past, people who want you to come over to their house and look at the slides of their vacation, people who get a couple drinks in them and just want to talk about their high school days or ten years ago… Those are people who think it's a shame that they didn't capture their entire lives on video.

Focusing excessively on the past is just a way out of the present.

It's a bail-out. It's a flight. It's an escape.

And it doesn't work. It's never satisfying.

Living in the past, focusing on the people and events who you think caused you to be like you are, is not helpful. It's not resourceful, and it is not courageous. It's not creative, and it won't lead you anywhere you want to go.

One system that counters this is a process I learned from the great ontological teacher Werner Erhard. It's called "Creating the future from the future."

Most people try to create their future from the past.

They wake up, project the past up onto their artist's canvas, and then add little touches of color to it here and there. But by focusing this way on the past, the only future they get (best case!) is a slightly-improved past. That's the best they can do.

Why not create your future focused on an exciting and thoroughly invented future? Why not create the future from the future?

Whenever someone comes to me for help, I listen very hard and ask myself, "What does this person really want—and what will they do to keep from getting it?"

~ **William Perry**
Harvard professor of psychology,
as quoted by Robert Kegan

Lie #15

That's just the way I am

This lie keeps you from getting the future you want.

And this lie is really interesting in the world of coaching, because it is the lie that comes from trying to maintain the illusion of a permanent personality.

In other words, I believe I've got this permanent personality, and "it's *just the way I am.* End of story!"

(Wait. Did you say *story*? Did you say end of *story*? You may be on to something!)

Did you quote your new bigger fee?

No.

Did you ask for the big, total package you wanted?

No.

Why?

Well, you know, I like to go slowly, that's just the way I am.

Did you call her?

No.

Why?

I'm shy. I'm an introvert! That's just the way I am.

People make up permanent characteristics for themselves, all the while cheerfully saying, "That's just the way I am."

But it's not really true. Your illusion about the way you are does not have any real permanence at all. And it certainly doesn't *cause* you to do anything.

If you had to be some totally opposite **other way** for some emergency reason, it wouldn't take you any time to be the other way. Heartbeat!

So the lie is, "That's just the way I am," and the truth would be, "That's just the way I *chose to be at that moment.*"

Let's say you were coaching people in a company and the president said, "We're going to have a big client appreciation dinner and I'd like you to be the greeter *and* the emcee. We're going to have a lot of our customers and clients come to the dinner and you'll be at the door. I want you to welcome the people. Your job will be to really make people feel welcome when they arrive."

What would you say to the president? "I'm a little shy, so when they come to the door I'm not going to really greet them. I'm not going to be able to look them in the eye, smile, and say 'Welcome!' like you want me to, because that's my personality, that's just the way I am. I'll probably have my back to them and be drinking deeply from the tequila bowl. I hope that's okay with you. There's nothing I can do about it because that's just the way I am. And as for being your emcee? Not possible. Again, it's the introvert thing. I can give you a book about it."

You would miss a chance to serve.

How I am right now doesn't have to be a result of a fixed entity I'm imagining called "me." How I am right now can be the result of a simple desire.

Let's say I have a burning desire to serve this wonderful company any way I'm asked. I want the president to appreciate my work and spirit.

So when he says, "Will you be the greeter?" I can say, "Sure, I'll be the greeter!" and even if my past history was not to be very open, smiling and welcoming to people, I will not care at all about that. Tonight, at the company dinner, I'll be a great actor! I will be a warm and welcoming greeter and emcee! I can play that.

All I ever have to ask myself is this: **Who do I need to be** to achieve my purpose?

That's the real question! That's the question that gives you access to your highest self.

And that's *more* authentic than people fixating on their imaginary permanent characteristics and covering their cop-outs with the pride of "authenticity" and "vulnerability."

Fixed personality people say things like, "*Because I am the way I am,* I never achieve my goals, I never keep my promises to myself or my family."

Because you have to keep your identity instead? Because it's just the way you are?

The truth is better than that.

When it feels like all the walls are caving in,
it's okay, we can let them fall.
Climb on top and we'll get higher.

~ The Ready Set

Lie #16

I'd love to do that, but I don't have the time

Time Warrior addresses this... All I can say is that when you become a time warrior this is a non-issue, forevermore. Get that book immediately if this is a lie you tell yourself.

Because, actually, Lie #16 is two lies.

The first lie is that **I would love to do it**.

Really? If I'd love to do it, I would do it. So it's not really true that I'd love to do it.

And it's also not true that I don't have the time to do it.

What is true?

THIS IS THE TRUTH: I have chosen not to prioritize it.

That's it. That's all there is in life. Choices and priorities.

If I were honest I would realize: "If it was a priority for me I would be doing it."

I do what I prioritize.

Everyone does what they prioritize.

No one only does what they have "extra time for."

But don't you hear this a lot? "I'd love to do that, but I don't have the time."

Just realize, from now on, that whenever someone says that to you they are not telling you the truth. The truth is really this: "That's not a priority of mine. If it were a priority, I'd do it."

A lot of times people in coaching say, "I'd love to do more research on my prospective clients, but I don't have the time. I'd love to have more conversations, but I don't have the time. I'd love to go out and see my clients and visit them on their work site, but I don't have the time. There are books I want to read, but I don't have the time!"

The truth is we all have time. We've just chosen **not to do** it.

And this is extremely good news, once we see it. Because we can start living at the level of choice, a powerful, fun level to live from! Try living at the level of choice.

We all have the same twenty-four hours.

The richest person in the world has the same twenty-four hours that you and I have. Not a nanosecond more.

We just have different priorities, and when we really see that bright truth, we can become more effective at building our coaching practices. We can now say this to ourselves: "Would going out and spending time with this prospect be a good use of my time? Would I get a high return on that activity, given what my overall goal is?"

If I would, I'm going to do it. If I wouldn't, I'm not.

Because I want my day to be filled with high-return activities, not random busyness and all the things that do not have any return for me.

Knowing and zeroing in on HIGH RETURN activities is one of the advanced client systems. It lets me do the things that I, myself, prioritize. There's none of this mental confusion about **I'd love to do it, but I don't have the time.**

In a vineyard, one grape will begin to ripen and in so doing will send out a vibration, an enzyme, a fragrance, or an energy field of some kind that is picked up by the other grapes. This one grape signals the other grapes that it is time to change, to ripen. As you become a person who holds only the highest and best for yourself and others in your words and thoughts, you will signal to all around you simply by who you are that it is time for a change. Without even trying, you will raise the consciousness of those around you.

~ **Will Bowen**

Lie #17

I'm helpless

Lie #17 is kind of a redundancy because it repeats all the other lies. It's the lie that's inside all the other lies. **It's the basic lie that all the other lies are versions of.**

And it's the lie that says I'm helpless.

That's the ultimate lie, because we human beings are anything but helpless.

We human beings have enormous internal spiritual and intellectual resources. We have energy resources that we feed off of whenever we make up our minds to do something.

You've seen it in your kids, you've seen it in everyone you've ever known; you've even seen it in yourself.

Every time you absolutely, without going back on it, make your mind up to do something, I defy you to think of a time you haven't done it.

So, therefore, in most cases, what's in the way of your success as a coach is a lack of *choosing* to succeed. There's a lack of devotion to your best life. There's no clean and clear inner choice that says **I'm doing this.**

When you make that quiet inner choice you hear a

wee little voice that says **I'm doing this,** and you now realize, "I can count on it, you can count on it, and the universe can count on it."

Helpless?

Anything but. Now help seems to blossom forth from everywhere. Are you really doing this? If so, the whole world's got your back.

Every single moment of existence
is a creative act.

~ Ken Wilber

About the author

Steve Chandler is the founder of the Coaching Prosperity School and its Advanced Client Systems programs.

He's the author of dozens of books, including the bestsellers *Reinventing Yourself, Time Warrior, Fearless* and (co-authored with Rich Litvin) *The Prosperous Coach.*

He lives in Arizona with his wife, Kathy, and their two canine companions, Jimmy and Hastings.

You may find him and sign up for free stuff at his website, www.stevechandler.com.

Books by Steve Chandler

Wealth Warrior
Time Warrior
The Life Coaching Connection
Fearless
The Woman Who Attracted Money
Shift Your Mind Shift the World
17 Lies That Are Holding You Back
10 Commitments to Your Success
Reinventing Yourself
The Story of You
100 Ways to Motivate Yourself
How to Get Clients
50 Ways to Create Great Relationships
The Joy of Selling
Powerful Graceful Success
RelationShift (with Michael Bassoff)
The Small Business Millionaire (with Sam Beckford)
100 Ways to Create Wealth (with Sam Beckford)
9 Lies That Are Holding Your Business Back
(with Sam Beckford)
Business Coaching (with Sam Beckford)
100 Ways to Motivate Others (with Scott Richardson)
The Hands Off Manager (with Duane Black)
Two Guys On the Road (with Terrence Hill)
Two Guys Read the Box Scores (with Terrence Hill)
Two Guys Read Jane Austen (with Terrence Hill)
Two Guys Read Moby Dick (with Terrence Hill)
Two Guys Read the Obituaries (with Terrence Hill)
The Prosperous Coach (with Rich Litvin)

Audio by Steve Chandler

9 Lies That Are Holding Your Business Back
10 Habits of Successful Salespeople
17 Sales Lies
Are You A Doer Or A Feeler?
Challenges
Choosing
Creating Clients: Referrals
Creating Clients: The 18 Disciplines
Creative Relationships
Expectation vs. Agreement
Financially Fearless
How To Double Your Income As A Coach
How to Get Clients (audiobook)
How To Help A Pessimist
How To Solve Problems
Information vs. Transformation
Is It A Dream Or A Project?
Making A Difference
MindShift: The Steve Chandler Success Course
Ownership And Leadership
People People
Personality Reinvented
Purpose vs. Personality
Serving vs. Pleasing People
Testing vs. Trusting
The Creating Wealth audio series
The Fearless Mindset
The Focused Leader
The Function Of Optimism
The Joy Of Succeeding
The Owner / Victim Choice
The Prosperous Coach (audiobook)

The Ultimate Time Management System
Time Warrior (audiobook)
Welcoming Every Circumstance
Who You Know vs. What You Do
Why Should I Reinvent Myself?
You'll Get What You Want By Asking For It

The Coaching Prosperity School and its Advanced Client Systems

Steve Chandler's six-month school for coaches focuses on the money. It's completely dedicated to systems and practices that lead to increasing a coach's prosperity.

The highly acclaimed book and audio *The Prosperous Coach* was co-written by Chandler and master coach Rich Litvin to offer to the world the unconventional principles and practices taught in this school.

Often referred to as "The ACS," the six-month program gives coaches three live weekends, two webinars a month, weekly peer coaching, a video practice-building tip each day from Steve, and much more.

The school is not a school for people who want to learn to become a coach. It is not a certification program. It is for people who are already coaching and want to learn to build their practices financially.

Some of the many hugely successful graduates of this school include Michael Neill, Carolyn Freyer-Jones, Rich Litvin (attended four times), Stephen McGhee, Michelle Bauman, Brian Whetten, Ron Wilder and many more.

Further information about attending the school can be found on the www.stevechandler.com website.

BONUS CHAPTERS FROM

WEALTH WARRIOR

The Personal Prosperity Revolution

Steve Chandler

MAURICE BASSETT

books for athletes of the mind

Introduction

How to create worldwide prosperity

I honestly believe it's one person at a time.

I know that may sound naïve as big nations keep moving vast sums of borrowed money around trying frantically to keep their treasuries afloat.

How could one person counter that?

But recently a client of mine told me about one person. One person donated a gift to his small college in the midwest. And it was an anonymous cash gift of $100,000,000. Yes you read that right, one hundred million dollars.

Steve Jobs was one person, and look at all the wealth (and jobs) he created. True, too, with Mark Zuckerberg at Facebook. He was one person, one nerdy college student in a dorm creating a network for the school to connect with online.

Creating.

A woman I know is a wonderful actress. She could have remained simply an actress forever, but instead she divined a mission to teach women to become amazingly strong, sexy and fit through pole dancing. Sheila Kelley. The S Factor Workout. Check her out.

Although S Factor now employs hundreds and serves tens of thousands, Sheila Kelley started it from zero. Nothing. And now all this.

Sheila, too, is one person.

I myself pay various coaches, designers, event planners, airlines, bookkeepers, accounting people, etc. I pay them money and add to their prosperity. They serve me so well. And I am able to pay them because my books, my training, my coaching and my seminars sell. In fact, my books sell in China. China pays me for that... China pays one person.

Our government *borrows* money from China just to make the interest payments on its own out-of-control debt. But I don't borrow from China. The money China sends me is for *work* I have done.

I don't owe China anything.

They owe me. They pay me.

I am one person.

You are one person.

We can create worldwide prosperity one person at a time.

The warrior's approach is to say "yes" to life: "yes" to it all. We cannot cure the world of sorrows, but we can choose to live in joy.

~ Joseph Campbell

Chapter 1

How could I possibly make any money given my past history?

Life's tough. It's tougher if you're stupid.

John Wayne

I had two alcoholic parents.

I had a wife with a medical disorder who was hospitalized and who left me with four children to raise on my own.

Those were my excuses. And you have to admit they're pretty good. Pretty dramatic. How could you ask someone to overcome that?

How would someone ever learn to create wealth with those kinds of things to deal with?

Wait. It gets worse. (Or better, depending on where you're coming from.)

I had (what I thought was) a birth defect. I was missing a gene that most humans had. It was the gene that provided you with a work ethic.

People talk about a "work ethic" as if it's a quality like blue eyes. You either have it or you don't.

I didn't have it.

How can you make brown eyes blue? With contacts? Too temporary and irritating.

That's how I felt about my work ethic as I emerged from

high school—clueless about how I could make a living.

Would I go to college?

Of course! Not because I wanted to learn anything or do anything with my college experience. But because it would buy me some time away from having to work.

We are all somewhere on the developmental ladder. And most people are growing, and, yes, ascending.

Except for me.

I was stuck. No upward development for me. Development did not look fun. It looked like work.

Little did I know that the secret to growth and wealth was less than a heartbeat away.

I just couldn't feel my heart at the time.

It's easier to build
strong children than
to repair broken men.

~ Frederick Douglass

Chapter 2

My perfect escape from work and adulthood

Like I said, my high school years featured no work ethic at all.

My grades barely allowed me to graduate. I certainly couldn't get in to the University of Michigan at Ann Arbor where all my friends were going. So rather than go to a lesser school in Michigan I chose to go for some wild adventure: the University of Arizona! Great party school, far from home. The perfect escape from work and adulthood.

Except that even at the University of Arizona you had to show up for class, turn in your homework and take your finals. And that was beyond my capacity. To put forth that kind of effort? No way did I know how to work that hard.

So drugs and alcohol became my answer. I would take drugs to study (supplying chemically the energy I was incapable of generating on my own).

And it worked. But really? It didn't. Because of the alcohol part. Way too much alcohol that wild freshman year.

A friend of mine and I knew that campus may not be a good place to study for our finals. Too many distractions were there.

So we rented a cheap hotel room in Tucson, far away from campus. A yellow motel out on Miracle Mile, with a nice pool. We thought we could really focus on our final exams there.

And it was actually working for awhile. In fact, our plan might have succeeded except for one thing.

The alcohol.

We got far too carried away with the weapons-grade, 180 proof pure something or other we had bought in Mexico, and it wasn't long before we'd decided to forget the books and instead stage a water ballet for the guests at the hotel pool.

Although we were thrilled with our performances in the pool, I'm glad it wasn't filmed because I'm not that good of a swimmer, and I'm sure if the guests got any value from the show it was all the unintended comedy.

My friend and I failed our final exams—especially the ones we didn't show up for.

Which in my case was all of them.

When the letter arrived home back in Michigan all our suspicions were confirmed: this kid has no work ethic. He is SUSPENDED from the University of Arizona due to bad grades. He has one more chance next year to prove he can study. Another failure will result in his being banned from attending this fiesta college forever.

Banned from attending a great party school? How sad and weak was that?

Of course my father was appalled and embarrassed, but not actually surprised. He had identified my lack of ability to make any kind of sustained effort very early on in my life. My chores were never quite finished. My grade school teachers said I was the laziest they'd ever had.

"Why did we ever think college was a good idea for him?"

"Because what's the alternative?" my mother would ask my father. "A job?"

And they both dissolved into laughter. Oh no. No way can we picture this boy holding down a job.

So it was back to college. And this time I was scared. Because I got the message. If I failed this time, I would have to learn how to work for a living. Unimaginable to me. That was an impossible scenario that I wasn't about to put to the test.

No, I would learn to stay in school. The answer would be in a *wiser* use of drugs and alcohol. This time, when exams were coming up, I'd back off of the alcohol and increase the use of amphetamines.

Who says I can't learn anything in college?

I learned to stay in school!

Barely, though. Just barely.

Because although I was not kicked out ever again, it was three years before I achieved the rank of sophomore. My parents were getting nervous because their friends' children were all talking about going back to Ann Arbor for their senior year. Some would be going on to law school. Many already had jobs lined up.

And here they were unsure if I'd ever become a sophomore.

By this time I began to acknowledge that there was something seriously "wrong" with me.

My alcoholic drinking had become my real job. I didn't "know" I was an alcoholic, but I was.

And it would get worse before it got better.

A sense of entitlement guarantees that eventually you will see yourself as a victim.

~ **Ezra Bayda**

Chapter 3

No ambition, no goals, no dreams even

It is better to have a permanent income than to be fascinating.

Oscar Wilde

Why am I telling you all this?

How can this story about my life possibly make you rich?

Hey, just trust me.

This is important: When you add alcoholic drinking to no work ethic, you get zero achievement.

I'm sure this isn't news to you. Everyone knows someone who has been caught up in this no-win kind of loop.

And let me just mention here that although I now have thirty-some years clean and sober through the grace of God and a beautiful 12-step program, I do not see sobriety as particularly heroic. I'm very grateful for it, but it's not a highlight on my resumé.

I see celebrities and politicians' wives getting standing ovations on TV talk shows for their newfound sobriety. Here, let me stand up and applaud you for going a certain amount of days without falling over drunk! Heroic!

Not to say I don't admire people in recovery, because I certainly do. They have found the courage to change the things they can and the serenity to accept the things they can't. No small thing.

But in my case it was important for me to get real about all of this and understand what a truly heroic effort was all about.

So in recovery I decided I would have to achieve the serenity that came with accepting that fact that I was born without the ability to work.

Not only that, it was worse. I had no ambition, no goals and no dreams. Nothing. Just empty when it came to all that.

Who knows why, really? I now know it wasn't genetic. I now know that *work ethic can be built from nothing, and even strengthened at will.* But back then?

It might have been my growing up with hugely successful (by the measure of money and social status) alcoholic parents. What was the lesson there? For a small boy? Work hard and become successful and you'll be drunk and depressed for the rest of your life?

Who knows what beliefs took hold in the brain of a very impressionable young boy?

And when it comes to creating a good life, beliefs are the only problem.

Why tell you this sad history of mine? Because there is something great inside all of this. Something I might even call the heart of the wealth warrior message: IF I CAN DO THIS ANYBODY CAN.

Chapter 4

Work ethic and the wealth it produces can be built and strengthened?

Back to the exciting news I kind of jumped over before: work ethic can be built and strengthened.

That would soon become my breakthrough.

That would be my life being handed back to me after all those years. I'd been alone for so many years with my lack-of-achievement gene. To realize that there was *no such thing* was nothing short of a rebirth for me.

I finally graduated from college. After only twelve years! A bachelor's degree in creative writing (what's that?) with a minor in political science (huh?).

But before you start mocking me for having taken twelve years to get a bachelor's degree, please know that I took four years off from that hero's journey to join the army. And I had great adventures in language school (the Defense Language Institute), doing electronic spying on the Russians while in Berlin. After that I was on to psychological warfare. But still, even in the army, the missing achievement gene kept showing up.

I was honorably discharged, which was something. But my rank at the time was Private First Class. For those of you unfamiliar with the military ranking system, I won't go into any great detail about it, but I will say that taking four years to become a Private First Class is not a great achievement.

I'm sure you're thinking, *How is this underachieving guy going to teach me anything about making money?*

I think that's my point, though. I wanted to set this up just right for you. Please realize: if I can do this, anyone can. And in working with so many people over so many years who have experienced various similar levels of loserdom, I can report that it's true: anyone can do this. Anyone can *go warrior* and create prosperity for themselves.

But in order to make money you have to know who is doing the making. In my case, if it had to be that same "me" who was missing a work ethic, then it would have been a lost cause.

The same with you. Your sense and experience of *who you really are* is the first step toward making money. Because if it's going to be that old collection of hurt feelings and fears you call "you" then we're in for a rough ride.

For you to create wealth in ways that are free, imaginative and prolific, you have to have access to your higher self.

Higher self?

The real you—you at your best. You when you surprise yourself.

Don't you surprise yourself once in a while? That's the "you" I'm talking about.

That's the real you.

The rest is fears and bad memories.

At least, that's my experience and the experience of the clients I coach. What do I know beyond that? I am only an authority on my own experience. I'm not an authority on anything else.

But here's where it actually gets exciting. This old, struggling "you" is not natural or "real." Your higher self is the most natural "self" for you to be.

You were meant to thrive.

But you'll only find this out when you take action.

Made in the USA
Middletown, DE
07 June 2015